Ev<

I Will Follow God's Call

Encouragement You Need to

Overcome Your Fears

My Best Life Possible Series

Karen Wells

ISBN: 978-1461086680

"For I know the plans I have for you", declares the LORD, "plans to prosper you and not to harm you, plans to give you hope and a future."
Jeremiah 29:11

I dedicate this book to my wonderful husband Simon, who has been my strength, encouragement, and support throughout all the endeavors I have pursued for God. Not once did he ever suggest that my dreams were far-fetched or impossible to reach. He has held me up when my "knees were knocking" and been my faithful behind-the-scenes cheerleader.

Acknowledgements

God has provided some incredible support to me in order to see this book in print. I want to especially thank my editor Susan Lawrence, graphic designer Christine Dupre, and transciptionist Alma Noefe. What a super group of women to work with. (You can learn more about their services at the back of this book.)

I want to acknowledge Christian Women Affiliate (www.cwaradio.com) and their willingness to allow me to be part of their Christian Women Blog Talk Radio network. Had I not finally stepped out and started doing the radio show my book would still be "inside me."

I'd also like to give special thanks to my sister-in-law, Susan Maruzs, who has been an incredible inspiration and support to me. She has often expressed that what I have to share is very valuable and helpful. She continually encourages me to "get my message" out there.

Again, I acknowledge my husband Simon who has done enormous behind the scenes administrative work for me (not to mention a great amount of cooking and cleaning while I was glued to my computer). He has also spent numerous hours listening to me "talk things through". What a gift.

Of course, I need to acknowledge my God and Savior, Jesus Christ. The hope and joy He gives is the inspiration for my whole life. Without Him, there would be no calling to follow.

Table of Contents

Introduction

Following God's call can be scary. We're asked to step out, take risks, and try different things. But I've decided – no matter how fearful stepping out might be, I am going to follow God's call.

I've often felt my knees knocking as I stepped out to follow God. I've felt incompetent, uncertain, or a myriad of other things. I have many reasons for not following through as quickly as I could.

For example, I've had this book in my heart for a few years now, and I have to laugh to see that it has been some of my own fears that have kept me from seeing the dream of having this book published. Yet, this is proof that even though my knees were knocking, I can follow God's call anyway!

I have written this book to be an easy read – something you can get through in a short period of time. I want to help you get moving on your calling. After each chapter I have added a few questions for you to ponder. I hope you spend most of your time on these questions. As you search your own heart and situation, it is my desire that God will spur you on to movement for Him. Have a pen and paper handy, so you can jot down the many nuggets of hope and direction He is going to give you.

We all have stuff in our lives that might stop or slow us from following God's call. If anything is preventing you from following God, I pray He will help you walk through it so you can move freely and fully into His purpose for you. You can have the best life possible as soon as possible.

It's what God wants for you.

In Him, Karen

1
We Know Not Because We Ask Not

Sometimes we don't know God's purposes for our lives because we simply haven't asked. I've chatted with many women who say they want to do God's will, they want to be fulfilled, and they want to have purpose. Yet when I ask, "Have you asked God what you're supposed to do?," they often pause and admit, "No. I don't know what to ask. I don't know how to ask."

My heart is stirred, because I want every woman, including you, to know what and how to ask God about the purposes He has for your life. It's the first step in finding and living out all that God has for you.

We all have different purposes. God has made us unique, creating a plan for each of us to live in a way that grows the kingdom for Him. My plan will look different than your plan. The specifics of my life will be different from yours. But there are parts of God's plan that are consistent across all of our lives.

When you're unsure how to seek God's purpose for your life, you can always rely on foundational truths and direction He gives to all.

Love God

Jesus replied: "'Love the Lord your God with all your heart and with all your soul and with all your mind.' This is the first and greatest commandment." Matthew 22:37-38

We can be certain that as we love God, He will reveal Himself more and more to us. As we know God more, we become more familiar with the purposes He has for us. God promises that He will answer those who seek Him. The more you know God, the more you'll desire God, and the more God will use you to fulfill the purposes He has planned for you.

Center your heart and your decisions on Him. God gives us the desires of our heart. As you know

Him more, you become more familiar with the desires He has planted within you. Your thoughts become entwined with His thoughts. His will and your will become inseparable. How exciting that is!

When searching for God's purposes, it's imperative to love Him. Loving Him, putting Him first in all things, reveals His character and purpose to you.

Love Others

"And the second is like it: 'Love your neighbor as yourself.' All the Law and the Prophets hang on these two commandments." Matthew 22:39-40

Immediately after Jesus instructs us to love God, He tells us to love our neighbors as ourselves. He declares these two commandments fulfill the whole law. But what does it mean to love your neighbor as yourself? Jesus gave us a very broad understanding of what that might look like in Mathew 25:35-36, when He said, *"For I was hungry and you gave me something to eat, I was thirsty and you gave me something to drink, I was a stranger and you invited me in. I needed clothes and you clothed me, I was sick and you looked after me, I was in prison and you came to visit me."*

Now we have practical examples of what loving a neighbor is – meeting the needs of people. As we meet the needs of people around the world, God is glorified. We love God, and His love flows through us in service to others. In the process, we're growing in our relationship with God, and He's glorified.

You might still wonder about the daily practical "how-to" of what Jesus is telling us to do. You might want to ask Jesus, "What exactly do you mean about feeding you, clothing you, and caring for you? How do you want me to do that?"

Let's get specific. One thing you can do is look at your own circle of influence. What needs do you see around you? Perhaps there are physical needs. Perhaps you see established ministries serving in areas that stir your heart. Or perhaps you see a gap in how needs are being met and you have a vision for what could be. What are your experiences? How has God gifted you? What skills do you have? When you begin to put all these pieces together, what commonalities do you see? What pathway seems to be created in order for you to meet the needs of other people?

 You don't have to be afraid to ask God what His plans and purposes are for your life. God will never lead you astray.

When you seek and trust God, you will not end up somewhere you shouldn't be.

We sometimes get scared. I've heard people say, "I'm not going to ask God if I should go to the mission field because He might send me somewhere I don't want to go." Believe that God is not going to do anything or send you anywhere that is inconsistent with His calling or purpose. When we yield to Him, we trust His calling and purpose. Everything might not fall into the plan we have for ourselves, but through faith, His plan will be revealed.

When you accept the foundational truth and commands of loving God and loving others, you might still wonder "How do I find out what this is going to look like in my daily life?" How do I find the answers to my questions?

Prayer

The only way I know to specifically hear from God is by going to God in prayer. (Fasting might also accompany your prayers at times.) If you want to know the purposes God has for you, you have to talk and listen to Him.

This isn't the same as day dreaming about something or chatting with your girlfriend about things you would really like to do. It's fun to daydream, and chats with girlfriends are energizing at times; you don't need to cut these out of your life altogether. However, the only way to really know what God's call is for you is to ask Him and listen.

As you pray, talk, and listen, ideas will come into your mind and stir your heart. You will begin to see the needs that are around you. Often these will be things you've never considered or you feel ill-equipped to complete. Or, perhaps you've already considered something, and now you begin to see it more clearly.

I know from experience that listening takes patience and discernment, but it's worth the wait and effort.

Make a decision that you are going to carve out uninterrupted time in your life to be alone with God.

Go humbly and boldly before Him and I promise you that God will meet your heart's cry.

1. What needs do you see around you that stir you to want to be involved in helping?

2. What are you most afraid to ask God about in regards to His purposes for you?

3. What are your strengths, skills and giftings?

4. When and where will you carve out time to talk to God about the purposes He has for you?

2
Is It Too Risky to Risk?

When you ask God what He wants for you and commit yourself to being obedient, it feels risky. I assure you – and you'll learn this along your journey – that you're not going to lose anything important if you follow God's plan. As a matter of fact, you're going to gain from following God's plan.

Risking is a two-sided experience: It can be very exciting and yet fearful at the same time. As we risk, we realize failure is possible. In my opinion, fear of failing is one of the major stumbling blocks to risking.

The fear of failure actually has the power to cause us to say "no" to the possibility of pursuing God's purpose, or we don't even seek His purpose at all.

You might be thinking, "What if it doesn't work?" What if I step out and do something that makes me look foolish? We too easily get stuck in the "what if." It is the "*What if*'s" that keeps us from following purposes God has planted in our hearts. People often don't ask the "what?" and "why?" of God because they don't want to take the risk. They think they might not be able to succeed – and perhaps they won't by their own standards. But if it's God's will, and they're being obedient, they will succeed in His purpose for them.

I encourage you that failure isn't the real problem. Failure is when you fall down and you don't get back up.

Staying down is the real loss, not the falling down.

Many, perhaps all, people who have been used by God felt they've failed or faltered at some point. If they had given up, imagine the ministries that wouldn't exist and the needs that wouldn't have been met.

While risk can involve fear, it also involves excitement. Risking involves stepping out in faith and moving outside of your comfort zones, which produces great potential. That's the thing about the vision of God's plan – it includes the vast potential that only God can contain, see, and give.

Life is full of joys and disappointments - whether you're taking risks or not. If you step out and do something and it doesn't work out the way you thought it should, God isn't going to erase your name from the Book of Life. I don't' know about you, but this gives me the courage to do many things I wouldn't normally do on my own strength. I'm excited that I will be with my Lord someday. He's committed to a relationship with me and wants me to fulfill the purpose He has for me, and He's not going to erase my name just because I make a mistake.

Another truth I cling to, because God says it's so, is that my value is not equal to my accomplishments. I am who God says I am. I'm valued because God says I am. I am a 10/10. Let me explain:

I often ask women how much they love and value themselves on a scale of 1 -10 (10 equaling 100%). Most do not say 10. Numerous women say 1- 5, and others even give me a minus (-) number.

The truth is we are all 10/10 because our value is based on the fact that we are created in the image of God as a human being. That truth never changes. When we equal our value to our life experiences and character (I call this life growth stuff), we often punish ourselves because we see that our life growth stuff is far from perfect.

Our value and life growth stuff are not the same! No matter what you have done, what has happened to you, or what others say and do to you, your value is always a 10. Your life growth stuff might need some work, but not your value.

My value comes from the fact that I am created in the image of God as a human being. My accomplishments are only life growth experiences, not value-based experiences. My value will never change, no matter what I do or do not accomplish. This gives me the courage to step out in faith, not fear.

God doesn't look at the outward, He looks at the heart, and He has chosen to value us. God values you.

God also works out all things for good. *And we know that in all things God works for the good of those who love him, who have been called according to his purpose.* (Romans

8:28) Especially as you feel as if you're risking something, it's good to know there are great benefits to risking.

God will challenge you to grow as an individual – mentally, emotionally, or spiritually. It's important that as we live as Christians, we don't become stale. We want to grow as much as possible. As you risk, stepping out in faith in your relationship with God, He'll work in your life, often moving in miracles.

I could fill this book with incredible stories of my own life, as well as others' lives, about what happened when they stepped out in faith. God meets our needs, and He meets them in big ways only He can accomplish. He wants us to jump to Him in faith!

You don't need to be afraid to risk. You don't need to be afraid you're going to lose something you can't live without when you commit to God's purposes. God is trustworthy. Just seek Him and His purposes. I guarantee you that He will answer.

Yet, let's be honest. Sometimes we do ask, take the risk, move forward, and flop. What then? Was it not God's will, or did we somehow misinterpret what God was saying?

If you strongly feel God has called you to do something and He's given you clear direction, I encourage you to not give up too quickly. Life has ups and downs, and if we give up too easily, sometimes God's purposes will not be accomplished. He wants us to persevere when it comes to His purposes. As I mentioned earlier, think of the many ministries that wouldn't have impacted many lives through the years if people had given up with the first struggle or roadblock.

When you're confident in God's direction, but you're frustrated because something isn't going as smoothly as you'd expect, ask God to show you a different route or approach. Use the situation as another opportunity to seek, listen and be obedient.

I must admit…I don't easily give up on anything I'm confident God is leading me into and through. I suppose that's one of the reasons I'm adamant in encouraging you to strive to fulfill the dreams – the purposes – God plants in your heart. God doesn't give us dreams for us to experience emptiness. He intends to fill us up.

When I was around 24-years-old, before I was married, I shared with a pastor I trusted that I was feeling I'd like to get married. I will always remember what the pastor said to me.

"Do you think God has put that desire in your heart?" I replied, "Yes."

The pastor continued. "Do you think God would dangle a carrot in your face, kind of like you would do to a horse to get it to come to you but never give it to him? Well, God never does that."

Those words have continued to help me accept that if I have a dream in my heart, and I'm confident it was planted there by God, I'm not going to behave as if I believe God is just dangling something in front of me to make me feel as if I can't reach it. If it's God's will, He wants me to keep moving and reach out and grab it.

So, when you're discouraged, ask God how to refresh that original purpose He revealed to you and say, "Fear, get behind me!"

1. What vision have you let die?

2. Are you the type of person who usually plays it safe? Why are you afraid to risk?

3. What could be the worst thing that could happen if you stepped out in faith and it did not work out?

4. Do you believe you are a 10/10?

3

'Fess Up

We know our deepest faults. We know our areas of weakness. As Christians, we're taught that we're saved by grace, not by works, but sometimes we feel we've done something impossible – or at least improbable – for God to forgive. We keep hold of these things, choosing not to confess them to God, which would then allow us to move forward.

I encourage you to stop hiding whatever it is you feel God can't or won't forgive. He already knows, and He's waiting for you to bring it to Him. It's probably fairly heavy as you carry it around. Just 'fess it to Him!

As I've grown in my faith, I've learned I can talk to God about anything. It's definitely not always easy, but since He is already aware of what's going on in our lives, what's holding us back?

I talk to many women who feel stuck in life. They're often ashamed of themselves. It seems simplistic, but I tell them "If you've done something to offend God or someone else, just 'fess up!" We get paralyzed by hiding something in the darkness. We spend most of our energy trying to cover our tracks. It's a difficult way to live life.

I frequently work with post-abortive women. Many post-abortive women I've talked to haven't come to full healing. They haven't accepted God's grace. In the meantime, they're standing on the sidelines of their own lives. God has purpose for them, but they're not participating because they're not stepping into the reality of truth and accepting all that God has planned: His forgiveness, His grace, and His purpose.

I also work a great deal with women who have been affected by someone else's sin against them. This includes women who were sexually abused as children, or have been in relational abuse. Although the actual trauma was not the woman's doing, often the outcome of how they are coping with the trauma affects their relationship with God and others. Women can become bitter, angry, withdrawn, and depressed.

I don't know what your life is like right now. I don't know what you've done or where you've been, but I'm certain of one thing.

God can forgive everything.

1 John 1:9 says that *"if we confess our sins, he is faithful and just and will forgive us our sins and purify us from all unrighteousness."* No exceptions.

Please don't let a past sin, trauma, or anything else, stop you from getting everything worked out with God so you can fully embrace His purposes for you. Get excited about what He can do in your life. God is loving, and He's ready to fulfill His purposes through your life…today.

To help women move beyond past trauma and pain into the purposes God intends, I offer the *Unhooked! 7-Steps To Emotional Freedom* counseling program. You can learn more about my telephone counseling services at www.mybestlifepossible.com. No sin is too great to be forgiven. No trauma is too deep to be unhooked.

If you or someone you know is stuck in a past trauma or sin that has led to feelings of shame and unworthiness, the 7 steps included in this program help women to move beyond their paralyzed state. 'Fessing up helps unhook people. 'Fessing up frees people.

I am a living example of being freed. That's why I'm so passionate to help free others. If God can turn my life around, He can turn anyone's life around – including yours.

So don't be afraid to go to God. God never wants you to be afraid to 'fess up to Him. He is always approachable. If you feel afraid of going to Him, you're hearing Satan, not God. Satan wants us to be afraid of God. He wants to keep us from serving God. Satan wants us to believe God doesn't care about us and won't forgive us.

Satan is a liar. He's the enemy, and he's trying to pull you away from God. Fight him. Challenge what Satan is telling you. Replace his words with the Word of God.

Then go humbly and honestly before Jesus. You will be free. God intends for you to be free. Freedom is a gift. Open up your heart and fully embrace the gift of freedom God has for you.

1. Is there something you are hiding from God?

2. Do you believe there are levels of forgiveness?

3. What could be the best thing that could happen in your life if you dealt with your sin or were freed from a past trauma?

4. Do you know how to discern the difference between God and Satan's voice?

4
Spiritual Eating Disorders

Sometimes our eating disorders hold us back from pursing God's purposes for us. I'm talking about spiritual eating disorders.

Just like natural eating disorders, spiritual eating disorders are serious and difficult to recognize. The symptoms of eating disorders often go undetected until a time of crisis.

If someone struggles with anorexia, you might not notice until the disorder has significantly progressed, because her weight might change gradually, and you often won't notice other health-related issues. Someone who has bulimia might keep her patterns of binging and purging well hidden. However, in both situations, the person's body is suffering. Even when early signs go undetected outwardly, there is internal harm being done.

The same is true in our Christian walk. We're often very effective in hiding how we're doing in our daily spiritual walk. As I refer to spiritual eating disorders in the context of our Christian walk, I'm not referring to outward activities. I'm talking about the things people can't see as easily, what we do behind closed doors, such as our daily intake of the Word of God, worship, and prayer.

Are you an anorexic Christian? Do you eat the Word of God in tiny bites? Do you restrict your reading of the Word of God?

What often happens when you're weak and tired and you're faced with trials is that you have difficulty focusing. You can't discern God's words from something the enemy might be telling you.

If what I'm saying seems familiar to something you've experienced, it's time to learn how to grow beyond the anorexia of your spiritual life. Begin by reading the Word, worshiping, and praying regularly.

I'm not talking about legalism. I'm talking about heartfelt, regular desires to read God's Word. Our lives are busy, and we have to make choices in how to fill our time and our bodies. Physically, we know we need to eat regularly. We need to eat healthy. Yet, we may neglect what we know we need. The same thing happens with our spiritual life.

You have to be intentional about your spiritual diet.

It might take more time, but the investment is worth it. Others might judge you or try to pressure you to fill your time, mind and soul with junk food; they might tell you you're being selfish. But feasting on spiritual food, regularly consuming the Word of God isn't selfish. Nourishing yourself regularly with the Word of God will make you strong and healthy.

We might feel that we must be active in order to be spiritual. Spiritual obedience and maturity does involve action, but we can't expend energy in activity unless we're properly nourished. Relying on insufficient nutrition leads to exhaustion or short-lived bursts of energy.

God pours nourishment into you as you feast on His Word. Feasting on God's Word requires that you not only read regularly but that you learn to read it in a way that seeps in. When studied well, God's Word will infuse your life with guidance, challenges, and provision.

Some people read their Bibles regularly, and God will bless the time they spend in His Word, but if they're legalistic about it, focusing on the task more than the relationships, they're approaching the Bible as an anorexic approaches food. It's a tool, an obligation, perhaps even an obsession, but it's not a healthy relationship.

I often hear people say they don't understand the Bible, it makes no sense to them, it's boring, it's not relevant for daily life…the list goes on and on. I encourage them to dig deeper. Research different approaches to studying the Bible, various styles of Bible studies, and Bible study tools.

Perhaps you can begin with an ABC study. Have you heard of ABC studies? Already Been Chewed. These are the tried and true studies written by people who have chewed through the Word of God and recorded their reflections, helping those just starting in Bible study learn the basics of the experience. Perhaps they've written in devotional form, so the reader can ingest bite-size pieces of God's truths.

You can also take a journalistic approach, which is one of my favorites. I'll choose a Scripture or a book of the Bible, and I'll be the journalist, asking who, what, when, where, why, and how. I read a portion, stop and ask such questions as

Who's involved?

What can I learn about it?

When can I put this into practice?

How can this affect my life or someone else's?

Why should I be doing this?

I like the journalistic approach, because it's consistent with the way I think. It's important to find a good fit as you explore study options.

Another study technique is expecting God to guide and provide each time you study. You might choose a book of the Bible and then you trust God will reveal whatever it is He wants you to hear within that context. You sink deeply into whatever you've committed to study. You read the designated book or section every time you've set aside time for devotions and studies each day. You begin to read, and the moment something jumps out at you, as if God is highlighting it, you stop. Instead of continuing to read, you meditate on what jumped out to you. Talk with God about it. Feasting on the specific meal God is giving you for that moment is another way you won't become spiritually anorexic. Let God feed you sufficient bites that keep you more than barely alive.

The goal is eat regular, healthy portions of the Word of God to be spiritually healthy. For some people, spiritual anorexia isn't tempting, but spiritual bulimia is.

People who binge eat large quantities of food and then make themselves sick so they won't feel overwhelmed. In order to draw spiritual connections, I'm not going to say we make ourselves sick when we binge on the Word of God. But when we try to cram excessive doses of God into our lives in a short period of time, not because we're seeking Him in healthy ways but because we're trying to fill something that's unfulfilled, our "full" feeling isn't going to be healthy nourishment. It will often result in that uncomfortable "ugh" feeling, making us overwhelmed, wanting to get rid of the feeling and claiming "I've had enough to last me for a long time. I'm taking a break."

When we're honestly seeking God, we're going to rely on Him to give us healthy doses. We're not going to rely on our own sense of spiritual body image or fullness. We'll let God determine what we need based on our spiritual metabolism, dietary needs, and thirst.

Be balanced as you seek the wisdom of God's Word. Remember, the goal is to know His purposes and figure out how to follow them. If you're spiritually anorexic or bulimic, I encourage you to reconsider the spiritual suicide you're committing.

Spiritual eating disorders result in uninspired hearts and unfulfilled lives. But when you balance your study and prayer time, when you have healthy spiritual habits behind closed doors, God will fan your heart's spark into a flame.

As the fire of the Holy Spirit ignites in your life, you'll begin to identify and step over the stumbling blocks that would want to stop you from God's purposes. The journey becomes thrilling. And I want you to experience the thrill!

1. Are you an anorexic or bulimic spiritual eater ?

2. Do you have a specific tool you use for studying God's Word?

3. Do you feel like devotions are a "time waster" because you have more pressing and practical things to be doing each day?

4. Do you journal your time with God so you know exactly what you have "eaten"?

5

Know Thine Enemy

It's important to know who you can trust and who you can't. I'm not just talking about people. I'm talking about God and Satan.

God highlighted something to me when I was reading several years ago: The greatest way that Satan wins is by getting people to believe that God is the enemy.

The statement jumped off the page at me, and it's helped me through the rough spots of life. When I wasn't sure whether or not God's purposes in my life were working, this statement came back to me to help me discern if what I was hearing was from God or if Satan was trying to trick me, luring me away from God.

Be honest. When things aren't going well, is your immediate response usually to blame or question God or do you still completely trust Him?

Satan is thrilled when we blame or question God. He'll do whatever he can to take our focus off of God. Satan wants us to blame God for the negativity, evil, and difficult stuff in life. Satan wants us to be angry with God, considering God as our enemy.

Of course, God isn't the one we should blame. He's not an accurate target of our frustrations, anger, and disappointments. He'll walk us through them. He's patient as we work through the rough spots. He'll help us move on. God isn't the enemy. Satan is.

We often have a double standard. Life can be going smoothly, and we get so caught up with the joy of life that we don't give God enough glory. Then things go poorly, and we give Him all the credit, or blame.

I encourage you to remember this statement: "God is not my enemy."

I know you're probably thinking, "Of course, God isn't my enemy. I don't believe He is, and I don't tell others He is." But I challenge you to think beyond what you say or even believe. Consider what you live out; what does your everyday behavior say about what you believe when things are not going well?"

Do you mutter to God, "Why is this happening? Why won't you make this different? I prayed for two hours about this and then I get up off my knees and everything falls apart. Don't you love me? Don't you care about me?"

These are the types of comments, thoughts, and questions that Satan wants you to think. Remember, he wants you to believe God is your enemy. It's difficult when you're in the rough spots of life to weed through these questions. It's important that you learn to recognize what's from God and what's from Satan, so when you're faced with trials, you can better discern truth from lies.

Be aware of your thoughts. Thoughts, particularly when they're based in lies, will pull you away from seeking God for the purposes He has for you. Your thoughts will divert your attention away from God's path through the trials, and you can easily get stuck. God doesn't want you to get stuck.

God wants you to move through a struggle and work through it within the context of your purposes.

He'll use what you're experiencing even if you can't or don't see a connection.

> We don't have to understand everything in order to trust God.

Instead of clinging to God more tightly through struggles, we often pull away and walk away with a heart full of frustration and anger. I'm certain you know people who are angry with God because they experienced a trauma or trial and blamed God. They built a wall between themselves and God to avoid getting too close to whom they believe is their enemy instead of running closer to Him for comfort as a best friend.

The truth is all good things come from God. No evil comes from God. All things don't go perfectly while we live on earth, because we live with sin, which has consequences. Life is messy. And Satan uses that messiness as he strategizes how to pull our attention away from God and believe lies about Him, such as

God is our enemy. So we believe the lies of the liar, Satan. The real truth is that Satan is the enemy!

I know this is an intense struggle for many women, and I hope these words encourage you. Remember to declare, "God is not my enemy."

Let this truth pull you toward God. Let these words be a reminder through your negative thought patterns. Let these words challenge you to release your anger. Satan is the one who deserves our anger. You can cast all your anxieties and anger far away by giving them to God in the name of Christ. Ask God to help you declare and believe only His truths and toss away any lies of Satan. Satan is your enemy. God is your friend.

1. Do you feel Satan is trying to trick you or lure you away?

2. Are you in the habit of blaming God when things go wrong?

3. Do you consciously examine your thoughts to be certain they are not lies?

4. Do you live in anger towards God?

6

What Fingers, Lingers

Anger is cancerous. As we learned in the previous chapter, anger can easily separate us from God. Many other misdirected emotions can easily have the same effect.

When we hold on to ungodly feelings, such as resentment, jealousy, bitterness, hate or unforgiveness, we begin to filter everything that happens in our lives through those feelings. We strain our experiences through filters that skew reality. As we linger in negative, unhealthy emotions and thoughts, we can easily become bitter, jealous, resentful., and unforgiving.

Our negative emotions end up spawning more negative emotions.

As we linger on negative, unhealthy emotions and thoughts, we create habits, and our negativity becomes familiar and comfortable. It begins to feel like reality to us because it's what we know well. We experience it over and over, so we rest on the reliability of negativity – even though it's cancerous and is slowly, destructively working through us.

We become so accustomed to the negativity that we might not even recognize it. When we keep resentments, jealousies, bitterness, hate and unforgiveness in our hearts, we begin to ignore such emotions are there. We no longer see them.

People around us see the negativity. They experience the negativity. They might even confront us on it. We'll likely respond, "No, I'm not bitter. How dare you say that!"

Sometimes we'll even deflect the confrontation, and we'll point to someone else, blaming her for the negativity. We use what emotions linger to point the finger toward someone else. As we repeatedly blame people, our hearts are hardened. Perhaps we're not negative 24/7. Sometimes we compartmentalize much of our negativity to a particular person or situation, and as time passes, all negativity gets funneled toward the single person or situation – even when there's no relationship.

If you find yourself struggling with negativity within a particular relationship, and you feel you don't have the same struggle with anyone else, ask yourself if you're allowing negative and unhealthy emotions to linger, causing you to point the finger at a particular person. If you find a connection, reverse the process. Point the finger back at yourself and ask yourself what negativity is lingering. Acknowledge you're struggling with thoughts and feelings that are harming you, your relationship with others, and your relationship with God.

We can't fully recognize and fulfill God's purposes for us if we're harboring sin in our hearts.

When we're harboring negative and unhealthy emotions, we're harboring sin in our lives.

It's not an easy thing to hear, but I'm just repeating what God's Word says. If we don't know the truth, we can't live by the truth.

God doesn't want us to be walking around in a mode of ministry or service with a mess of horrible feelings in us. When someone looks into your eyes, God wants them to see Jesus, not a bundle of messy, unhealthy, stale emotions that have been lingering for years.

God doesn't want you to get rid of these lingering unhealthy emotions because He's condemning you. He loves you and wants you to be healthy. He's passionate about you and wants you to live out your purposes. And He knows in order to do that, you have to leave the junk behind. He'll help you determine what's junk and what's not, what's unhealthy and what's healthy.

It's so important we get our hearts right with God. If God is speaking to you right now, please take the time to get on your knees and talk with Him. Humble yourself before God. James 4:10 says *"Humble yourselves before the Lord, and he will lift you up."*

Humble yourself. Let God clean up the junk in your life. As you get the junk out of your life, you'll be able to move forward in healthier spiritual living. I know you'll enter an exciting chapter of your life as you leave the junk behind. As you do, you'll encourage others to do the same.

That's why I have hope for you…because I've experienced this personally, and I want to encourage you through my own experiences. I don't have it all together, but side-by-side, we can all go to the same cross – to find and completely rely on Jesus.

I share these things because I want to see more Christians free for God's purposes. I come to you with a heart of humility and compassion. I believe with my whole heart that if Christians are free, they will change the world!

When we're bound, we have little impact on the world, because we can only go as far as our chains allow.

But when we're unbound, we have freedom. Freedom to touch the world beyond the chain length. Freedom to fully access and live out God's power and purposes.

I've walked to the cross repeatedly because I've realized something I've said or done hasn't been beneficial to myself, people around me, and my relationship with God. I need to take everything to God as quickly as possible. God forgives me. He accepts me. He loves me. And He sends me onward in His purposes for me. Isn't that thrilling?

Look at your heart. Take whatever you need to be unleashed from to God. You can touch the whole world for God in His plan for you. What more could we ask for?

1. Are you judgmental?

2. Do you need to forgive someone?

3. Do you have chains around you that are stopping you from moving further in life?

4. Do you play the blame game?

7

Put Away the Hammer

As I'm counseling women, I listen to them punishing themselves, beating themselves over the head, and I tell them to "put away the hammer."

> There's no benefit or value in beating yourself up.

Despite the tragedies you've survived or the things you've done, you will not get healthy by punishing yourself.

We often rationalize that self-punishment makes us feel better or that it helps us deal with what has happened in our lives, but I want to assure you self-punishment is not God's answer to struggles.

God gave His Son, Jesus, to die for us. Jesus suffered for us. He was punished for our sin. We have consequences for the sin in our lives, but we have no necessity for self-punishment. When we take on the punishment, we're behaving as if we're not accepting Jesus' sacrifice. We're assuming the power that only He has.

Because of Jesus, we don't have to live under a belief system of works; we don't have to work our way into or punish ourselves before God gives us freedom. That's not how God works. It's not who He is.

God gives us an avenue for the support and healing we need. He removes the guilt and shame from us. We don't have to punish ourselves for it. He's waiting to take it away. He longs to give you freedom.

Keep in mind there's a difference between true guilt and false guilt. False guilt and shame is from the enemy. It's not God-focused. It looks inward. It's self-degradation. It's connected to hopelessness. It's feeling guilty about things that you have no need to feel guilty about. You begin believing that you're unfixable, and you get stuck in a place you feel you can't get out. That self-condemnation is not from God. He wants freedom for you. Self-condemnation is Satan's condemnation.

However, there is true guilt. We have to let God define what guilt and shame is instead of believing lies about them. God's guilt is conviction. There are similarities of emotional experiences between true guilt and false guilt, yet it's essential to discern the differences in the reality of the situation.

When you experience guilt, and you're uncomfortable in your heart about something, the first thing you should do is look to God. When you look first to God, you'll be seeking His truth and His perspective. He's the best reality check you can have.

If what you're experiencing is true guilt, you will not begin to degrade yourself. You'll humble yourself before God and take all that you need to Him. You'll find hope. You'll find opportunities to heal and grow in the freedom only God can give you.

Be on your guard, because false guilt and shame often wears a cloak to make it appear as if it's from God. Remember, Satan is deceptive. I've talked with many women who have been in emotional, physical, sexual, or mentally abusive relationships. They often carry around a heavy burden of false guilt, believing it is true guilt. They don't know they can give it over to God. They don't know there's a difference. They don't know how to move on. So, they continue to punish themselves with the hammer.

Put away the hammer. Kick the condemnation out of your life. Listen to the convictions of God. Move on in His freedom.

Be encouraged with the possibilities of knowing the difference between true and false guilt. Be prepared to find the difference between the two. When you find yourself looking inward and degrading yourself, claim it's not from God. Let the Holy Spirit convict you of anything separating yourself from God, including self-punishment – and move forward in His purposes for you. God wants you to fully experience His freedom.

1. What do you "beat yourself up" for?

2. Do you believe you are "unfixable"?

3. Can you tell the difference between condemnation and conviction?

4. Are you carrying heavy burdens in your heart?

8

To Teach is to Be Taught

In order to know and follow through with God's purposes, we need to be teachable. Being teachable is imperative. We cannot move forward in God's purposes with haughtiness or stubbornness. You might get somewhere in your own effort, in the flesh, but it will likely not be where God would take you in the Spirit to fulfill His purposes for you.

Being teachable is humbling. Being teachable is learning to hear other people's perspectives, because none of us knows everything. It's about being pliable and not jumping to a judgmental conclusion and response.

Of course, everything you learn will not necessarily be the specific direction God has for your calling so you need to sift through what you are hearing. So, I encourage you to have mentors. I encourage you to get involved in groups or organizations where you can share what you know. As you share, you'll compare new information with the basis of truth you, and others, already have. You'll discern.

Listen to others who have a passion for seeking and knowing God's purposes. Gather wisdom and insight from their experiences. Share your own. As you build relationships with like-hearted people, you'll teach and be taught.

Jesus taught that it is important to be teachable. *This is why I speak to them in parables: Though seeing, they do not see; though hearing, they do not hear or understand. In them is fulfilled the prophecy of Isaiah:*

> *"You will be ever hearing but never understanding;*
> *you will be ever seeing but never perceiving.*
> *For this people's heart has become calloused;*
> *they hardly hear with their ears,*
> *and they have closed their eyes.*
> *Otherwise they might see with their eyes,*

hear with their ears,

understand with their hearts

and turn, and I would heal them."

But blessed are your eyes because they see, and your ears because they hear. For truly I tell you, many prophets and righteous people longed to see what you see but did not see it, and to hear what you hear but did not hear it. Matthew 13:13-17

Jesus will not use us to the fullest extent if we are not teachable. We must be teachable for Him, willing to listen. We need to open our eyes and ears so we can gather wisdom and live by it. We need to always be learning and growing.

> If you wonder whether or not you're teachable, just ask someone close to you who you trust. Don't worry, they will tell you.

They'll help you gain insight. Listen to them courageously and embrace the insight they give you.

A final word of caution for those who are vision-oriented and entrepreneurial. We can easily get blind-sighted and run ahead of God. We like to think in a forward motion, and risk choosing to see only our own priorities over God's. But when we're teachable, God will correct us along the path.

When you're teachable, you can learn something new every day. Isn't that exciting? Look forward to it. Each time you learn, realize you're growing. Embrace the learning process. Have a teachable spirit and God will continue to use you more and more.

1. Are you pliable?

2. Do you have an accountability partner?

3. Do you run ahead without getting advice and support?

4. Do others say you are teachable?

9

Signs Don't Always Drop Out of the Sky

Sometimes I look for answers to drop out of Heaven before I'm willing to trust that God is calling me to a specific purpose.

I'm not referring to the confirmations we receive as we pursue and accept His direction and instructions. We need to discern God's leading. We need to be certain what we think we're hearing from God lines up with His Word. We know that if something isn't going to honor God, He's not going to lead us into it. We need to check with God to be sure that what we perceive to be our God-given passions, desires, and purposes are actually God-given. We must continually seek and listen to Him.

When we're certain we're centered in God's purposes, we are not easily dissuaded when people say, "You don't know what you're doing. Why would you pursue that?" When you know…that you know…that you know God's purposes, you're determined to persevere…not because you're selfishly stubborn but because you're focused on listening to God and doing what He wants.

This type of conviction and confirmation is different than expecting a sign to drop from Heaven.

When I refer to signs dropping from Heaven, I'm suggesting we need to not sit and wait for something to happen, expecting God to make every move when He expects our obedience.

There are practical steps we need to take to be sure we're actively pursuing God's purposes.

We need to make plans. We need to pay attention to how our plans are going and how they're working into or away from God's purposes. We need to look for learning opportunities. We need to look for specifics in the process of following God's purposes.

I've often experienced that sometimes I need to apply or sign up for something, enroll in a program, or join an organization to take the first step in the direction of God's purposes. God teaches me every step of the way.

Something very special and impactful happened to me early in my Christian walk. I had always wanted to go to Africa. Even as a little girl, I wanted to go to Africa. I didn't have a specific reason; I just knew I wanted to go. Once I became a Christian, I started praying about going to Africa. I learned about Youth With A Mission, and I thought perhaps it could involve travelling to Africa.

We had an incredible youth group I attended every week. We spent a lot of time praying, including monthly all night prayer vigils. Several of us would pray through the night, seeking God's direction. My prayers always included, "Oh, God, should I go to Africa? Oh, God, I want to go to Africa. Please send me to Africa, God." Every month, I expected a clear answer from God: "Yes, go directly to Africa. Yes, Karen. You're going to go to Africa."

I remember one time in particular, I desperately began to bargain with God, "Okay, God, if I don't hear from you this prayer time, I am not going to Africa. I'll know you don't want me to go. I'm just going to give up this dream." I prayed, expecting an obvious sign from Heaven to be dropped in my lap.

I was begging God to send me to Africa in some big and obvious way. Instead, He prompted me with a simple thought: "Apply."

"What? Apply? What are you talking about?"

God made it clear what should have been obvious all along. If I didn't apply to Youth With A Mission and let them know I wanted to go to Africa, how would they ever know?

Not that He couldn't, but it was unlikely that God would tell someone in Africa, "Hey, there's a girl named Karen in Canada who's praying to come to you." God certainly has the power to drop signs from Heaven, so please understand I'm not saying it doesn't happen. I'm only saying we can't expect Him to always show up that way. We need to watch for the small nudges as much as obvious revelations. We need to listen for the whispers as much as the shouts.

God often nudges us in practical steps, such as the need to apply. I applied. Hearing from God in an unexpected way and being obedient even though it wasn't the path I expected changed my life. I learned something very important.

It's okay to do practical things while seeking God's calling.

I don't have to feel it's irrelevant to do something that seems too practical to be spiritual – like applying to Youth With A Mission. I was uncertain at the time. I didn't have a lot of confidence, but I completed the application. I was scared. I was intimidated into doubt, thinking they'd write me to say, "Are you kidding? You don't fit our criteria. Your Christian walk isn't mature enough. You've done this and this and this, which clearly disqualifies you for this kind of service."

God taught me to expect Him in unexpected ways, and He also taught me to trust Him through the process of following His purposes. When I submitted the application and had doubts and fears, God reassured me to stop worrying. I knew He wanted me to follow through. I knew He wanted me to learn something. So I persevered.

I went to Africa, and it was incredible. God planted the dream of going to Africa in me as a little girl, I learned how to trust Him through the process, and I grew immeasurably while I was in Kenya.

God has planted some kind of passion in your heart. If it requires an application or training, step out and do it. It might not seem spiritual enough for you when you consider it has to do with God's purposes.

> The practical can also be spiritual when it has to do with God.

It's God who makes something spiritual.

You might experience a sign dropped from Heaven at some point in your life, and experiencing God's supernatural intervention is amazing. However, you need to pursue God's purposes at all times, whether you're receiving signs dropped from Heaven or not. God shows up in the practical, too. Take the step. Make the move. It might be just the thing that propels your journey and purpose.

Since taking that first step in going to Africa, God has done many things in my life that I attribute directly to my practical pursuits. I've spoken to groups of women. I've taught and preached. I've travelled. I lived in China. I attended college and seminary. I started a business. And it doesn't stop. God continues to lead me. I'm continuing to do very practical, everyday things to explore and prepare me for His purposes.

I encourage you to take a step. If you make a mistake, you might end up walking down the wrong road, and that's okay. It's not the end of the world. Remember, God isn't going to erase your name from the Book of Life. You risked and stepped out for Him. You sought His purposes and took action.

I've messed up plenty, but I have to keep life in perspective. God focuses on eternity. Our focus should be the same. Seek God's direction and courage as you step out. "Go and apply."

1. Are you waiting for some "heavenly sign" before you will pursue your passions?
2. Is there something specific you need to sign up for, or join, in order to move into your passions?
3. Do you feel practical actions are not spiritual enough?
4. Are you looking for practical ideas to present themself?

10

Build Your Treasures in Heaven

How do we balance making certain God gets all the glory for those things we accomplish for Him, and yet become "known" in the ministry in which we are called? I've often heard people in ministry question whether or not they should publish a book or release a worship or speaking CD. They're concerned with the attention they might receive – that it will pull attention away from God.

I hear the concern, and if someone knows she's going to struggle with the personal recognition and not point the ministry back to God, it might be a valid concern. But the truth is if God purposes you to have a ministry, He is likely providing an avenue for you to get the attention so that people know you're available for ministry.

Being unwilling to accept the attention God is giving you so you can point people back to Him can stifle the purposes that God has for you.

I have a radio show on Blog Talk Radio with Christian Women Affiliate. If nobody listens to the radio show, what's the value of me doing it? By hosting the show, I'm getting attention. The women who hear me get to know me and, hopefully, begin to trust me. They're encouraged by what they hear, and perhaps they'll contact me to dig deeper and pursue the purposes God has for them. But if I shied away from any and all attention, I wouldn't be hosting a radio show, and women wouldn't be aware of some tools for them to heal and grow toward God.

When God is leading you in His purposes, you must follow. As you do, you are building treasure in Heaven like Jesus taught: *"Do not store up for yourselves treasures on earth, where moths and vermin destroy, and where thieves break in and steal. But store up for yourselves treasures in heaven, where moths and vermin do not destroy, and where thieves do not break in and steal. For where your treasure is, there your heart will be also."* (Matthew 6:19-21) When God plants a vision in your heart and you pursue it, you're building heavenly treasure.

We put too much emphasis on being concerned that others will judge our motives. I don't know your motive is and you don't know mine. While I can tell you my motive is to be extremely pure in what I'm doing, you can't know that for sure until you see the evidence in the way I'm living. If someone hears me on the radio or sees me involved in another area of ministry, and they think my motive is to get attention, I can't do anything about it.

I can't control others' assumptions. All I can do is cling to what's true and be obedient. I need to trust how the Holy Spirit is leading me, including keeping my motives in check and guiding me to store up treasures in Heaven for God's glory and never for my own.

If you're constantly worried about what others think about you, you will likely be held back in your full purposes God intends for you, because you're letting others guide your decisions. Don't yield that kind of power to others. God is the only one who can handle that level of power.

If everyone responded through the doubt of what others would say, we would be void of many blessings.

We'd miss out on most Christian books, CDs, etc., because no one would be fulfilling their callings in fear of being judged by others as self-focused.

Remember the children's song "This Little Light of Mine"? It says, "Hide it under a bushel? No! I'm going to let it shine!" Let's not hide our ministries and callings under a bushel. If we hide our purposes under a bushel, no one's going to see them. God won't be able to fully use them.

If you have concerns about what others think, or you're concerned about your own motives, take it to Jesus. He knows your motives. Check with Him and move forward. Every day we wait is another day someone might have heard what you have to share, but the longer you wait, the more others will miss out. Trust God's timing, and know that someone – perhaps someone you don't personally know – is probably praying for your ministry to come into their world today because they have a need you can meet.

Since making Karis Counselling Services more visible with the website, more teaching, having my radio show, etc., I've received numerous emails from people who have said, "I want you to know your message came just at the right time. I was praying for the answer you provided." Some have told me that I am a "God send". Others have told me that I have saved their lives!

I don't mention these comments to boost me up, but it's exciting to know God is using me. I love how He gives me affirmation and confirmation from those I'm ministering to.

I want you to know there are women in need who are longing for what you can give them. Trust God's timing, and step out. God gave you the gift, and He intends you to use if for Heavenly purposes. Don't be ashamed of what He has called you to. He has a plan for you to share His love with the world. Today's the day to build your treasures in Heaven!

1. Are you afraid of being noticed for fear of looking worldly?

2. Do you have a "treasure" in your heart that God wants you to build?

3. Are you worried about others judging your motives?

4. Are you hiding your light under a bushel?

11

Dressing for the Season

At one time, I didn't dress for the seasons. I'm not talking about clothing. I'm referring to the seasons of life.

I like seasons, because I like to see things moving all the time. Adjusting to changes can be a struggle, however. Perhaps you've experienced the challenges of adjusting through seasons of life. It can be exhausting because just as you adjust to one change, another change suddenly happens.

Time can seem like the enemy, but in reality, it's your friend. Time gives you the opportunity to do what you need to do.

Just like the seasons of winter, spring, summer, fall, we have certain activities we need to accept in the seasons of our lives in order to make each season the most productive it can be.

In winter, we must shovel. If you don't shovel, you get stuck. In case you don't know, I live in Saskatchewan, Canada. We don't have snow 12 months of the year, but we get a lot of snow. I got stuck in the snow this year. I learned. If you don't shovel, you get stuck.

In spring, you must transition to a different kind of clean up. The snow melts, but there's a lot of garbage and debris to clean up. Perhaps you clean your garden to get ready for planting. Spring cleanup is essential for productivity.

Summer comes, and while it might seem to be more relaxed, it's important to maintain. If you don't cut the grass, you might have unhappy neighbors. You have to water flowers, or they'll die. Summer is a time of growth, but you have to manage the growth.

And then comes fall, and it's time to rake the leaves. Then the wind comes along. More leaves fall. More raking. More wind. More leaves. More raking.

Fall can be the season of monotony. But it's also a time of preparing for the colder weather when you won't be able to take care of everything as easily.

Each season has its benefits and its necessities, so I encourage you to accept it for what it is and embrace what it requires, so you complete the purposes of the season before the next season arrives.

We often begrudge the season we're in because of what it entails. We want to get to another season, but once there, we begrudge it as well.

We often define the seasons of our lives in context of our roles and responsibilities. For example, I see some of my seasons as a mom, wife, employee, etc. Instead of living out these seasons with purpose and positive perspective, we can think of some it as time wasters. We don't want some aspects of the season. We begin to dread the season in its entirety because of the portions of it we don't want.

I used to think "I don't have time for this." I was unproductive through seasons of my life because I got trapped in the negativity. Because I chose not to be positive and productive, I didn't make the most of the purposes God had for me. Thank goodness, I've grown. Now I try to shovel, clean up, maintain and prepare in God's timing of my seasons of life.

When we don't enjoy the seasons we're in, we can end up with impatience and inactivity.

Impatience

You can detect impatience in your life if you hear yourself repeatedly asking "When will this happen?"

For example, when I married my husband (who, by the way, I deeply love), God had promised me we'd be preaching and teaching together as a couple. It was very clear to me this would happen. I had my idea what that would mean and often felt impatient when I did not see the fulfillment as I expected.

I've heard myself say, "God, you promised me that this is what we're going to do, but...." I'd get impatient. The truth is God didn't tell how we would be ministering together. He just stated we would. God has actually allowed many opportunities for us to minister together, and it has been wonderful; yet because I was impatient for what I *thought* it looked like, I did not see what was right before my eyes. I have learned to cling to the promise and accept God's timing and His way of fulfilling the promise. I now watch for the seed God has planted to grow, and I do what it takes to water and care for it as God leads.

There is a time for sowing and reaping, and there is also time in between. I didn't want to wait. I felt I was wasting time. That's impatience. In reality, the time I thought I was wasting was actually part of the sowing and reaping process. Patience is essential for growth. Once I realized that, I started relaxing a little bit.

There are still times I feel like I'm a hamster on a little wheel, working so hard to make things happen but going nowhere. I get stuck in the cycle of accomplishment, and in the process, I get frustrated and impatient, but I have to remember the process of sowing and reaping.

I've seen this process work in my life, because I've seen that sowing and time for growth can result in plentiful reaping. The reaping is often in becoming the woman God wants me to be in a certain area.

The growth process, the one I get so impatient with, develops me and prepares me.

I've experienced sowing and reaping in my role as a mom. Now, if you're a young mother, I know daily life can be challenging. You might wonder when you'll get to fulfill many of the other purposes God intends for you. I encourage you not to be frustrated in the season of raising your children. God will use each season to prepare you for the next. You can even begin to water some of the seeds in preparation – what I call fulfilling your purposes on a part-time or slow-time basis.

For example, let's say you're confident God is calling you to be a writer. I'm using this example because when my children were little, I felt writing was part of my calling. At first I felt frustrated, because I often didn't have time to write. But I began to see other ways I could prepare to become a writer. I enrolled in online courses about writing, and what I learned in those courses kept me engaged in my calling while also preparing me.

Now, years later, I'm writing this book. If I hadn't taken the time and opportunity to learn along the way, I'd likely not be where I am in the process of fulfilling my calling. I wouldn't know many of the things I'm using in the process of writing and publishing. And it started with me deciding to accept my season of life.

Whatever season you're in, be careful not to assume you're wasting time or that there's no progress happening. God is growing you for the season when you'll fully experience His calling. Of course, callings change and develop so you're always going to be going through seasons. You might as well relax along the way.

Inactivity

We can become inactive through our seasons of life. Inactivity often happens when we think a season is unfair. Have you ever felt something was unfair? I have. I've said, "God, this is unfair. I have all these plans, yet I'm stuck in this season. I don't like it."

Here's the problem with the "It's unfair!" attitude. We can make more work for ourselves because of our season of inactivity. We settle into inactivity, which includes no growth, no organization, and no planning.

The inactivity slows down the process of growing with God, so when we should have been ready for the next season of life, we're not.

We're in a holding pattern, because we've chosen to pout in inactivity.

There is a saying that states you can only lead someone as far as you have gone yourself. Each season leads into another. What happens in one season is the foundation for the next. When you choose inactivity, you choose not to build, which means there's no foundation for the next season. You can't jump ahead and build on something that's not there. You have to build one step at a time, so you might as well get active and start building.

When you try to skip steps in building, you'll end up spending most your time in repairs later. You might think jumping ahead in order to avoid wasting time now is a great option, but if you don't take the time your current season deserves, you'll likely spend even more time in repairs later.

I've talked to women who are at A and they want to be at C, but they don't want to do B. I assure them they have to do B and that they can't skip ahead. I assure them they'll get to C, which is their goal, but they have to move in order: A, B, C. Jumping from A to C simply won't work. Instead of being inactive through a season, get busy and do what needs to get done.

> Whether you struggle with impatience or inactivity, the reality is when we don't understand the seasons of life, we're in danger of losing our passion for our calling.

This is the saddest thing I see. When the opportunities come, our passions have died. Perhaps we won't even recognize the opportunities. There are too many women who aren't experiencing fullness of life because of discontentedness through seasons of life. Do not get caught up in an "all or nothing" perspective.

I don't want you to miss out, so I encourage you to dress for the seasons of your life. Don't begrudge them. Work for and through them, and in the end, you will reap what you sow.

1. Do you feel that "time" is your enemy?

2. Are you impatient with the sowing and reaping principle? What season in life do you find the hardest to accept?

3. Are there steps you are trying to skip?

4. Are you in danger of losing the passion of your calling?

12

When My Legs Are Steady

As we begin the final chapter, I pray you've been encouraged by the tips and challenges I've given you. I hope you're in a different place than you were when you began reading the first page. My heartbeat is to help women to have the best life possible, and I'm confident we must get unhooked from some of our junk in order to move forward. I don't want to be stuck. I doubt you want to be stuck. So, let's help each other out of the ruts.

As you get out of your ruts, I have one more tip to give you. At some point, you're knees aren't going to knock quite as much. Your legs are going to feel steadier. And while you might immediately think steady legs will be a welcome change, I don't want you to be caught off guard.

Even though steady legs will be an improvement, it's still a change, and any change creates some discomfort and instability. Be aware of it, but don't be afraid of it. You're growing, and it's a good thing. You're making progress as you live out God's purposes for you.

Always be prepared to declare: *"I have fought the good fight, I have finished the race, I have kept the faith."* 2 Timothy 4:7

1. What are three challenges God has given you while reading this book?

2. What is the next step you need to take in order to get unstuck?

3. Are you ready to move forward, even though your knees are knocking?

4. Where do you see yourself in one year from now, in regards to pursuing the calling God has for you?

Endorsements

Christine Dupre is a professional freelance graphic designer. With a strong Christian faith and commitment to professional design, she offers over 20 years of talent and experience to meet marketing and advertising needs, both personal and business. Christine can be contacted at: cedupre@msn.com

Susan Lawrence edits, writes and speaks. She's passionate about pouring into women and loves to equip and encourage them. In addition to being involved in local women's ministry for many years, Susan has developed resources and coordinated trainings and networking for international ministries and denominations. For editing services as well as her two women's Bible studies, *Pure Purpose* and *Pure Emotion*, visit www.purepurposebook.wordpress.com.

Alma Noefe provides virtual assistance support as a general/medical transcriptionist with experience in transcribing webinars, radio shows, conference calls, recorded phone calls, and interviews calls (as well as doctors' clinic notes, surgical reports, and psychological evaluations). She can be contacted at aon_77@yahoo.com or Odesk.com for any transcription services.

Need A Speaker?

If you are looking for a keynote speaker, a workshop speaker, or someone to teach, Karen might be the woman for your next function. She's been teaching, speaking, and developing workshops for numerous years. She has a strong passion to help women find freedom so they can live the best life possible and follow God's calling in their life.

Some topics include:

- Even With My Knees Knocking I Will Follow God's Call

- Unhooked! 7 Steps To Emotional Freedom

- Assert Without Hurt: 5 Key Strategies To Gaining Respect In Your Relationships

- Blue No More: 4 Components Of Defeating Depression

- Overtaken by the Red-Faced, Blood-Boiling Moments: 5 Ways To Master Your Anger Now

- The Heart Of The Matter: 10 Reasons We Don't Forgive And What To Do About It

- Counseling The Abortion-Vulnerable Woman

- Abuse Is More Than Skin Deep: 5 Ways To Escape The Unseen Pain

- Abuse Is More Than Skin Deep: How The Church Can Understand And Respond To Abuse Against Women

If you have another topic that you would like Karen to share at your next gathering, please contact her to see if she can meet your needs.

Contact Karen at kariscounsel@gmail.com or Skype at karenwells1.

Free Woman To Woman Ezine

Sign up today at www.mybestlifepossible.com

When you sign up, you will receive the free audio download, "The Biggest Lie Women Believe."

For women wanting hope, acceptance and change today!

In This Issue

Woman To Woman
Welcome to this issue of *Woman to Woman*. I trust you will find it helpful and enjoyable. This ezine is written for women, by women. If you have an idea
for a topic that you would like to see written about, let me know. Your ideas and feedback are a valuable contribution to *Woman to Woman*. Send your ideas
to womantowoman@mybestlifepossible.com.

Also, a **BIG** welcome to all the new readers who have joined the *Woman To Woman* community these past two weeks!

You are on our list because you signed up for *Woman To Woman*. To change your subscription, see link at end of the ezine.

If you received this ezine as a forward from a friend and would like to have your own copy sent to your inbox, go to www.mybestlifepossible.com and sign up. When you do you will also receive the free audio download, *"The Biggest Lie Women Believe".*

Feature Article:
"Boundaries:
Where do you stand?"

When you sign up you will...

✓ Gain tips, tools, and strategies for living a healthy emotional and relational lifestyle

✓ Stay informed about upcoming workshops, tele-seminars/webinars, and live radio shows

Woman To Woman is sent out every two weeks. You may cancel your free subscription at any time. We will not sell, rent, or trade your email address for any reason.

95

Links to Karen's Services

For more information about the services and programs Karen offers through Karis Counselling Services please go to the following:

Website: www.mybestlifepossible.com

Blog: www.mybestlifepossible.com/blog

Woman To Woman Radio Show: www.cwaradio.com

Contact Karen:

Email: womantowoman@mybestlifepossible.com

Skype: karenwells1

Twitter: kariscounsel

Facebook: facebook.com/KarisCounsellingServices

facebook.com/KarenMarieWells

To order additional copies of *Even With My Knees Knocking I Will Follow God's Call:*

CreateSpace eStore:

http://www.createspace.com/3588185

Amazon.com:

http://www.amazon.com/gp/product/146108668X

Available from Amazon.com and other retailers.

About the Author

Karen Wells, holds a Master of Divinity with a major in Marriage and Family Counselling from Briercrest Biblical Seminary, which is located in Caronport, Saskatchewan. She is the founder of Karis Counselling Services, a service devoted to helping women regain the power they've lost because of a past traumatic experience. She is the author of the *Unhooked! 7 Steps To Emotional Freedom* counselling program. Karen wants to give you women HOPE. Life is too short to be stuck. She wants every woman to know God has exciting plans for them.

As a globally-minded woman, Karen offers her services by telephone, skype/webcam, and webinar. She also hosts her own weekly live call-in counselling radio show called "Woman To Woman" through Christian Women Affiliate (www.cwaradio.com). She also facilitates workshops, speaks, and writes.

Alongside her husband Simon, Karen also offers telephone counselling to couples through Karis Counselling Services and Walk Together Marriage (www.walktogethermarriage.com).

Karen and her husband Simon are the parents of two children, Angela and Dean. They also have two small grandchildren, Kale and Paiton-Jade.

Made in the USA
Charleston, SC
21 September 2012